Bentley and the Great Fire

a serial for all ages

The sequel to Bentley Finds a Home

Story by Nick Pintozzi

Illustrations by Guillermo Munro
with Connie and Nick Pintozzi

Text and illustrations copyright © 2004 Nick Pintozzi

All rights reserved,
including the right of reproduction
in whole or in part in any form.

First Edition

Bentley and the Great Fire
is the sequel to Bentley Finds a Home,
the first story in the *Bentley Book Series*.

This book is published by BentDaiSha, LLC.

Printing by Daehan Printing & Publishing Co., Ltd., Seoul, Korea

Library of Congress Center Control Number: 2004093438

ISBN: 0-9749465-2-4

This book is dedicated to anyone who perseveres when faced with adversity, inspires another to do likewise, and lends a hand to someone who needs help to prevail.

While in Helen's arms at the birthday party, Bentley detects a problem elsewhere inside the Indigo Bush care home.

Chapter 1 – Sensing Trouble

    Bentley's eyes followed the flickering flames. From his vantage point, he could see all 100 candles. His ears perked up as he heard the singing of "Happy Birthday." All around him, there was happiness. However, he sensed there was something terribly wrong.

The celebration was in the activity room at the Indigo Bush Assisted Living and Residential Care Home, in central Tucson. It took place in autumn 2003 about three months after the wedding reception in the same spacious room for the home's administrator and its head chef. The birthday party was for Mei-Li, the eldest of the home's 24 female residents.

Bentley was perched in the arms of Helen. The retired photographer was regaining her strength after undergoing heart surgery. Beside her stood her friend Ruth, whose walker stood nearby.

When the singing subsided, there was loud cheering, then clapping. The noise nearly drowned out Bentley's sudden growling.

"Shush," Helen told the black-and-tan Chihuahua as the Chinese-American centenarian began giving a thank-you speech. But Bentley wouldn't calm down. Helen turned toward Ruth, excused herself and carried Bentley away from the celebrators.

Since discovering Bentley in Indigo Bush eight days before the wedding reception (he took advantage of an open window), Helen had never heard him growl like that before.

His first companion, however, had lived with him for two years and learned to recognize his warnings. Miss Lucy, who passed away four months ago and who had never met Helen, had pointed out that Chihuahuas have a keen sense of hearing. One of the many things the retired schoolteacher read to Bentley was that a dog can hear sounds 250 yards away that most people cannot hear beyond 25 yards.

As Helen walked toward the door to the hallway, she carried Bentley past a pet carrier containing another growler, the black-spotted-on-white Chihuahua named Daisy. Only about half the size of the 10-pound Bentley, Daisy had become friends with Bentley since being introduced to him at the wedding reception. Although her growling wasn't heard by the people standing around the birthday cake, Daisy did her best to make sure Helen heard it.

Helen did not know what to make of the two dogs' growling, but she knew she had to get Bentley out of the activity room, one of whose walls still bore a large jack-o'-lantern banner left from the Halloween party the night before.

Bentley was squirming as Helen carried him through the doorway, leaving a roomful of partyers, including Indigo Bush residents, staffers, volunteers, and visitors.

After taking Bentley into the long hallway and stepping toward the one-story care home's East Wing, Helen saw Bentley lift his nose and sniff the air. Helen did not smell anything unusual. But, as Miss Lucy had read, Chihuahuas have a highly developed sense of smell – perhaps up to a thousand times better than a human's.

Bentley sensed there was trouble beyond the hallway, which linked Indigo Bush's two matching wings. He increased his wriggling, forcing Helen to set him down on the tiled floor. He ran down the hallway, barking before he reached the carpeted East Wing.

Helen stood motionless in the hallway, puzzled by Bentley's behavior. She had never heard him bark like that before. Miss Lucy had pointed out, however, that Chihuahuas make excellent watchdogs and that their variety of barks includes what's known as "the alarm."

Bentley kept barking. At what, he wasn't exactly sure. But he had heard something. And he had smelled something. Now he was on his way to see something.

Even though he was a part-time resident at Indigo Bush, Bentley felt that Indigo Bush was his home. He had taken refuge in the old building when he fled the abusive 11-year-old twins of the couple who adopted him from the Humane Society of Southern Arizona after Miss Lucy passed away. At the wedding reception, he learned that his new companions would be the bride and groom.

Bentley and the Great Fire / Ch. 1 – Sensing Trouble

Bentley enjoyed living with Julieta and Bryan. She was Indigo Bush's head administrator, and her husband was Indigo Bush's head chef. Bentley also enjoyed accompanying the twentysomething newlyweds each day when they went to work at, or just to visit, Indigo Bush. In their own home, Julieta and Bryan treated Bentley like family, just like he was treated at the care home.

Besides Indigo Bush's elderly ladies and the newlyweds and other staffers, Bentley's buddies included Julieta's 8-year-old niece, Gabriella; Bryan's 9-year-old nephew, Tyler; the care home's eightysomething volunteer handyman, known as Mr. Fix-it; the red-haired teenage volunteer helper, Abigail; the middle-aged Tohono O'odham music man, known as the Chief (a weekly piano-playing visitor to Indigo Bush); and Pastor Connie, the fortysomething cleric who was accompanied by her Chihuahua, Daisy, on visits. Except for Helen and Indigo Bush's eightysomething Juanita (who had a headache and was asleep in her room), they all were at the birthday party when Bentley entered the East Wing.

Helen began walking toward Bentley but lost sight of him as he ran past the doors of the East Wing's 12 rooms and entered the relatively short hallway that led to the exit.

Bentley kept his brown eyes peeled for any movement. As Miss Lucy had read, dogs have a wider field of vision than humans (about 240 degrees versus 180 degrees) and can sense motion much better.

Just as Bentley reached the exit door, it swung open. Bentley was startled upon seeing a young person holding a metal can containing a liquid with a smell that Bentley recognized as gasoline. The burly teenager was startled upon seeing Bentley, who began barking as loudly as he could. The hairs on the back of Bentley's neck rose, and he bared his teeth.

"You got a lot of nerve!" yelled the teenager. "You're just a rat-dog," he added, swinging the can at Bentley.

The glancing blow to the head stung Bentley, but he was able to see the gloved attacker shut the door and run away upon hearing the screams coming from the hallway.

"Fire! Fire!" shouted Helen as she saw flames outside the window of the East Wing's adjacent storage room. "Bentley, come here now," she added, shuffling toward him. She reached down to lift him, but stumbled and fell, twisting her right ankle. The seventysomething woman in the dark-purple pantsuit lay helpless beside the momentarily dazed Chihuahua as the flames began entering the care home.

Bentley soon regained his bearings. He licked Helen's forehead and looked into her violet eyes. She understood what he was going to do. She patted him on his head before he began racing back to the activity room to sound the alarm.

Next: Into the Flames

Bentley and the Great Fire

**Defying the hallway flames, Bentley races to the room
of the remaining unevacuated resident in the care home.**

🐾 *Paw Prints: During a birthday party at Indigo Bush, Bentley sensed trouble elsewhere around the care home. He went to investigate and encountered a teenager who hit him with the gasoline can used to set the building on fire. While the arsonist fled, Helen, the resident who had followed Bentley, twisted her ankle and fell beside Bentley, who shook off the can's sting and began racing back to alert the partyers.* 🐾

Chapter 2 – Into the Flames

Bentley sped through the East Wing's day room and entered the long hallway, but before he could reach Indigo Bush's activity room, he was forced to make a detour.

The sound of footsteps on the wooden floor in the care home's entryway drew Bentley into the good-sized room, where he began barking loudly.

"You again?" grumbled the teenager holding the red can that had already glanced off Bentley's head. "I don't have time to keep messing with you," he added, dumping the rest of the rectangular container's contents onto the upholstered love seat before Bentley lunged at the left pant leg of his black jeans. "Back off, dog!" he yelled, lighting a match and igniting the sofa.

The fiery outburst halted Bentley in his tracks, and the youth with the long-sleeved plaid shirt escaped through the front doorway. Bentley turned away and ran to the hallway and on toward the open door to the activity room.

When Bentley returned to the birthday party, he barked but found himself competing with the noise from the lively singalong at the activity room's piano. As the Chief went through a flurry of keystrokes, Bentley ran to Bryan, who was standing away from the piano. Bentley jumped up against the right pant leg of the chef's white uniform.

"What do you want?" Bryan asked, looking down at the restless pet. "Come here," he added, squatting and reaching out toward him.

Bentley backed away and barked. Three deep barks, to be exact – what Miss Lucy had labeled "the alarm."

Unlike Bentley's first companion, Bryan did not know what to make of Bentley's behavior. Bryan stood up and turned toward Pastor Connie. "Bentley's acting strange," he told the woman with the short, blond hair.

Bentley barked again, took a few steps toward the door to the hallway and returned to his starting point.

"Are you OK, Bentley?" Bryan asked. "Where's Helen?"

Upon hearing the woman's name, Bentley barked again and stepped toward the doorway.

"What's going on?" Pastor Connie asked, walking toward Bentley. "You want us to follow you? Is that it?"

Bentley headed for the doorway, looking back a couple of times to make sure Bryan and Pastor Connie were trailing him. When he saw they were, he ran into the hallway and stopped. He waited until he saw his two followers again, then turned and started running down the hallway.

"There he goes!" shouted Bryan as he began to walk faster. He glanced back at the petite woman dressed in black.

"I'm coming," Pastor Connie told the trim man with the white cap. "I'm right behind you."

Bryan began running but abruptly stopped upon reaching the entryway crossing. He stood awestruck, looking at the fire raging in the entrance room. When Pastor Connie reached his side, she acted similarly. They remained motionless and speechless until they heard Bentley barking. They then realized he had come back to see why they had stopped following him.

"We've got to act fast," Bryan told Pastor Connie as Bentley resumed running back and forth. "The fire is too strong in there for us to stop it. We've got to turn on the fire alarm, call 911 and get everybody out of the activity room."

"How about Helen?" Pastor Connie asked, looking at Bentley. "You could sound the fire alarm and follow Bentley, and I could make the phone call from your wife's office."

"OK, but let's do it now," Bryan said, turning away and starting to run after Bentley. He stopped long enough to flip the switch at the alarm box. The loud noise did not frighten Bentley. He had heard it before during the periodic fire drills in the old building.

Pastor Connie scurried into the head administrator's office and picked up the handset of Julieta's telephone, but there was no dial tone. The phone lines had been cut.

Meanwhile, Bentley zipped through the East Wing's day room and into the hallway leading to the exit door. Helen remained on the floor, holding her right ankle. "Thank God," she said upon seeing Bentley and hearing Bryan call out her name. "Bryan, the fire's coming inside!"

"I can see it," Bryan said. "What happened to you?"

"I fell and hurt my ankle. I can't walk."

"We're going to get you out of here," Bryan said, kneeling down beside the thin woman. "Put your arms around my neck and hold on. I'm going to pick you up."

Helen followed Bryan's instructions. "I don't know how the fire started," she said as she was carried away from the exit door. "Bentley discovered it somehow," she added, looking down at the Chihuahua trotting alongside Bryan. "I followed Bentley here."

"I did the same thing," Bryan said, moving through the East Wing as swiftly as he could. "We've got to get back to the activity room. There's another part to the fire. It's in the front entrance. Don't look into the entryway when we go past there. Just hold on tight."

Bentley and the Great Fire / Ch. 2 – Into the Flames

When Bentley reached the activity room's doorway ahead of Bryan and Helen, he was met by Pastor Connie.

"The phones aren't working!" the clergywoman yelled out to Bryan. "We had to use a cell phone to call the Fire Department," she added before realizing Bryan was carrying Helen in his arms. "Helen, are you OK?"

"My ankle must be sprained," Helen said, clinging to Bryan. "I tripped and fell. I'll be OK."

"Good," Pastor Connie said before returning her attention to Bryan. "Julieta is seeing that the people in the activity room get out the back door, but she says Juanita wasn't feeling well and left the party early. Juanita must be back in her room in the East Wing near the exit."

Bryan turned around and saw the flames from the front room enter the hallway. Then he saw Bentley running into the flames. "Bentley, no! Stop!"

Bentley knew what he had to do. And the fire wasn't going to stop him from trying.

Next: Trapped!

Each caught in a ring of fire, Bentley and his friend Daisy strive to keep from giving in to the flames.

🐾 *Paw Prints: Bentley has discovered that a fire has been deliberately set at the Indigo Bush care home. He has confronted the arsonist, a teenager who has fled. Bentley has alerted the people inside Indigo Bush and helped rescue one of the home's residents. Now another resident needs his help.* 🐾

Chapter 3 – Trapped!

The flames in the entry room had flared into the hallway, but Bentley saw that the flames were higher up on the wall, so he was able to race down the hallway untouched.

The Chihuahua turned around in time to see Bryan run past a fiery flare. Bentley knew Indigo Bush's head chef would follow him because Juanita had to be rescued.

The eightysomething Juanita had left Mei-Li's 100th birthday party in the care home's activity room after complaining that her headache was worsening. She went to her own room to lie down. The native of Hermosillo, Sonora, was having a pleasant dream about her 4-year-old great-granddaughter, Brianna, when she was awakened by the fire alarm, which Bryan had sounded. She was groggy and disoriented. She slowly got up from her bed and inched her way toward her door. She finally managed to open the door but collapsed in the doorway, overcome by the fire's smoke.

By the time Bentley reached the doorway to the room nearest the flames in the care home's East Wing, Juanita was unable to hear his frantic barking. She lay unconscious in her light-blue housecoat, face down.

While the fire threatened to engulf the doorway, Bentley pushed against the left side of Juanita's back with his front paws, but he was unable to budge her.

During his three months as a part-time resident at Indigo Bush, Bentley had grown fond of Juanita, who was one of the two advocates for the care home's two dozen female residents. Likewise, the dignified-looking great-grandmother had grown fond of Bentley, to whom she often spoke in Spanish. *"Mi compañero pequeño,"* as Juanita called her "little buddy," was a good listener. His first companion, Miss Lucy, had habitually talked to him – both in English and (sometimes) in Spanish – during the first two years of his life, before she passed away.

As the flames moved closer to Juanita, the good listener heard Bryan's voice. "Juanita! Oh, no!" yelled Bryan when he spotted Bentley standing beside the prone woman. Bryan ran up to the doorway, fought off a flame with his bare hands and lifted the small, unconscious woman with his arms. "C'mon, Bentley, let's move it," he said, turning away from the doorway.

Meanwhile, in the parking lot behind the care home, the partyers who had been evacuated from the activity room watched as two fire engines and a ladder truck arrived and as up to a dozen Tucson firefighters began battling the blaze.

"Gracias a Dios," said Gabriella. "Thank God," the second-grader repeated.

"You can say that again," Tyler said, nodding his head. "The firemen did get here fast, but Uncle Bryan, Bentley and Pastor Connie haven't come out yet," the third-grader added in a worried voice while keeping his eyes trained on the activity room's exit door.

Gabriella looked worried, but she tried to follow her Aunt Julieta's example and not voice her anxiety. The pretty Latina admired the beautiful Julieta, who, as Indigo Bush's head administrator, had to appear calm and in control, even though her husband was among those still inside the burning building.

Gabriella, whose parents owned and operated a South Tucson tortilleria (which sold up to 300 dozen flour and corn tortillas a day), was a bright student with warm, brown eyes and dark-brown hair that covered half her forehead and extended beyond her shoulders. She was short and slender – and surprisingly strong.

Tyler, whose parents owned and operated an East Side garden nursery (which featured cactus plants), was an above-average student with bright, blue eyes and curly blond hair that was kept close-cropped. He was short and slender – and surprisingly impulsive.

To Gabriella's dismay, Tyler was about to demonstrate his impulsiveness again.

"How could you do that?" Gabriella cried out, glaring at Tyler after he unintentionally let the black-spotted-on-white Chihuahua get out of the pet carrier. "Daisy's heading for the fire!"

"Come here, Daisy!" yelled Tyler as he began running after Pastor Connie's tiny pet.

Like her friend Bentley, Daisy was attentive. When Daisy overheard that her companion and Bentley were among those still inside the building, she began furiously scratching the wire screen on Pastor Connie's pet carrier. Daisy kept up the grating noise until it became too much for Tyler to ignore.

Hoping to calm Daisy, Tyler unlatched the pet carrier, which he had set down on the pavement in the parking lot. He pulled back the screen a few inches and gently patted Daisy's head. Daisy, however, pressed her chest against the screen and extended the opening enough for her to climb out.

Free of the pet carrier, Daisy made a beeline for Indigo Bush's activity room. Tyler and Gabriella hollered for help, but Daisy was too quick for her pursuers. With the exit door remaining open, Daisy scampered into the activity room, the frenzied movements of her little legs a blur. She sped through the large room and neared the door to the hallway. Then Daisy heard the voice of her companion, who began walking into the activity room with Helen. Actually, Helen was limping after having sprained her right ankle.

"What are you doing in here?" asked Pastor Connie, shocked to see Daisy outside the pet carrier and inside the burning building. "Come here!"

Daisy ran toward Pastor Connie, but she stopped in the doorway when she saw Bryan carrying the still-unconscious Juanita. Overjoyed to see Bentley, who was farther back in the hallway, Daisy raced from the doorway toward him. Unaccustomed to running on the tiled floor, Daisy lost her footing and slid, passing by Bentley in the process. While she was regaining her footing, flames suddenly surrounded her.

Bentley realized Daisy was trapped. He also realized that he needed help to save her and that he couldn't get it from Bryan and Pastor Connie, both of whom were being ordered by firefighters to flee through the activity room's exit door with Juanita and Helen. Even before he realized it, however, another ring of fire surrounded Bentley. Now he was trapped, too.

Next: The Spirit of Service

After the spirited Sasha revives him, Bentley begins dragging the fire-weakened Daisy from the flames to safety.

🐾 *Paw Prints: Having already discovered the fire at the care home, confronted the teenage arsonist, alerted the other people in the home and helped rescue two of the home's residents, Bentley has become trapped in the burning building while on yet another rescue mission.* 🐾

Chapter 4 – The Spirit of Service

Bentley's friend Daisy was much shorter than any of the flames that surrounded her. The Chihuahua – not quite 9 inches high at her shoulders – ran around inside the tight circle, but she was unable to find an opening. A few feet from her stood Bentley, held captive by another ring of fire.

Bentley glanced back in the hallway and saw that there was no one at the doorway to the activity room. He had seen Bryan, who was carrying the unconscious Juanita, enter the activity room along with Pastor Connie and the limping Helen. He had heard men (firefighters actually) calling out to his companion and Daisy's companion. He thought Bryan and Pastor Connie would take Juanita and Helen out of the building and then try to come back for him and his friend.

When Bentley returned his gaze to Daisy, he saw the black-spotted-on-white pet collapse. Daisy – 18 inches long (including her 3-inch tail with the white tip) – lay motionless on the tiled floor in the ever-tightening fiery circle.

Bentley lunged forward in his own ring, but the flames forced him to turn back. He felt the fire closing in on him, and he slipped and fell. He was no longer able to see Daisy.

A few moments later, Bentley entered a dreamlike state – like the one he had entered about three months ago after he was grabbed by a coyote near the patch of prickly pear cactus plants behind Indigo Bush. With the help of a veterinary surgeon named Angela, he had recovered from that attack. In his unconscious state then, he had visited Rainbow Bridge, a place he had heard about from Miss Lucy. In certain veterinary circles, Rainbow Bridge was where pets who passed away went to be reunited with their companions. It was located, as his first companion once read to him, "just this side of heaven."

Unlike in his first visit to Rainbow Bridge, Bentley did not see green meadows nor pools of running water during his return. Also unlike in his first visit, he did not see Miss Lucy. However, like in his first visit, he saw a reddish Chihuahua with a name tag that read "Sasha." The small pet with the curled tail had the markings of a white diamond on her forehead and of white wings on her shoulders. A couple of months ago, Bentley had seen Sasha's image in a photograph. Sasha, who passed away more than two years ago, had been Helen's companion before Helen arrived at the care home.

As in Bentley's first visit to Rainbow Bridge, Sasha approached him during his return. Only now Bentley realized the stocky pet with the honey-brown eyes was standing between Daisy and him in Indigo Bush's burning hallway.

Sasha continued walking toward Bentley, passing through the flames that encircled him. She pressed her nose against his.

Suddenly, Bentley rose from the floor. He quickly squeezed through a narrow opening in the fire and reached Daisy. He wrapped his mouth around the back of her neck and swiftly dragged the unconscious, 5½-pound pet through the fiery hallway and into the activity room.

"There they are!" shouted a firefighter upon seeing Bentley and Daisy, who had just regained consciousness. Soon the fireman and another firefighter carried the two pets through the activity room's exit door.

Once outdoors, Bentley and Daisy were greeted by the cheers from their companions and the other people who had been evacuated to Indigo Bush's parking lot from the activity room, where they had been attending a birthday party for the care home's eldest resident, Mei-Li. Among the evacuees were representatives of the Tucson Chinese Association and the Pan Asian Community Alliance.

Bryan and Julieta ran to the firefighter carrying Bentley, and Indigo Bush's head administrator took the pet into her arms. Bentley licked her chin, and both she and her husband gently patted his head. "He looks good, doesn't he," the care home's head chef said, smiling. His wife, also smiling, nodded.

No one was happier to see Bentley than Helen, who credited Bentley with rescuing her after she twisted her right ankle and fell in the care home's East Wing. Bentley had led Bryan from the party to her side before the flames spread to where she had been lying on the floor near the East Wing's exit. Helen refused to get medical care until she held Bentley in her arms and saw that he was all right.

Meanwhile, Pastor Connie ran to the firefighter carrying Daisy. "She's mine," Pastor Connie matter-of-factly told the firefighter, who then handed the pet to her. "We'll need to have the veterinarian take care of these," she added, looking at the superficial burns on Daisy's front legs.

Tyler and Gabriella were relieved to see Daisy in Pastor Connie's arms. Bryan's nephew, who had unintentionally allowed Daisy to escape from Pastor Connie's pet carrier, sighed loudly. Julieta's niece, who had scolded him, quietly said a prayer of thankfulness.

Daisy was taken to the animal hospital where Angela was a staff member.

Bentley did not know how he had managed to get Daisy and himself out of the fire, but he thought that seeing Sasha had revived him. He remembered Miss Lucy reading to him about guardian angels and saying that they are spirits of service for the needy. That's what Sasha must be, he thought.

Although the fire at Indigo Bush was not great in scope, the damage was significant. Still, the firefighters had extinguished the two-part blaze before it had spread beyond the entry room and connecting hallway and the far end of the East Wing. An investigation had already begun.

Bentley had shaken off the glancing blow to the head from the gasoline-can-wielding teenager he had confronted at the East Wing's exit door and then in the entry room. The arsonist had fled, but Bentley could identify him for the investigators. The only problem was, Bentley thought, how would he be able to accomplish that?

At the moment, Bentley had other concerns. He was concerned about Helen, who was boarding an ambulance to get treatment for her sprained ankle. He also was concerned about Daisy. And he was concerned about Juanita, who had been rushed to the hospital by the Fire Department's paramedic unit after suffering smoke inhalation.

Those were more than enough concerns, but Bentley would have even more to come.

Next: The Day of the Dead

While in Julieta's arms, Bentley sees the framed photo near the shiny red apple on The Day of the Dead table.

🐾 *Paw Prints: In addition to confronting the arsonist and alerting the other people in the Indigo Bush care home, Bentley has helped rescue two residents and, with the dreamlike aid of a canine spirit named Sasha, has dragged his four-legged friend Daisy from the flames. Daisy has superficial burns on her front legs. One of the women, Helen, has a sprained ankle; the other, Juanita, has been hospitalized with smoke inhalation.* 🐾

Chapter 5 – The Day of the Dead

Bentley and the Great Fire / Ch. 5 – The Day of the Dead

The framed photographs stood on the small table at the home in Tucson's Barrio Anita. Bentley was easily able to see all of them from his perch in the arms of Julieta, but his eyes were drawn to a small, oval picture near the front.

Bentley was looking at an image of his first companion. His beloved Miss Lucy had often said he was smart. She would not have been surprised to know that Bentley, once Julieta began murmuring about *"esos perdemos,"* realized he was looking at images of people who had passed away. He scanned the other images. There was no photograph of Juanita among "those we miss."

The photo display was set up by Julieta in observance of *El Día de los Muertos*, the Latin American holiday that coincides with the Roman Catholic Church's All Souls' Day. *El Día de los Muertos*, or The Day of the Dead, is a celebration in which departed loved ones are remembered and honored – and their spirits are welcomed as guests.

If Juanita had passed away, her photograph would surely have been among those on Julieta's table because Juanita reminded Julieta of the young Latina's great-grandmother, who passed away at the Indigo Bush care home five years ago. Julieta had developed a close bond with her surrogate *la bisabuela*, who was one of the two advocates for Indigo Bush's residents.

Julieta had received the small picture of Miss Lucy from the family that adopted Bentley after Miss Lucy passed away. His adopted family, in turn, had been given the photograph by one of Miss Lucy's acquaintances, an elderly woman who happened to see Bentley with the family in a sport utility vehicle when she parked beside their SUV at a food store. In the conversation that ensued, the woman told the family how devoted Bentley was to his first companion. She persuaded the family's parents to let her mail them a copy of the picture of Miss Lucy.

The parents of Clyde and Callie – the abusive twins from whom Bentley fled – put the picture in a drawer. Julieta, however, found a frame for it and kept it on display in her and her husband Bryan's home in their predominantly Hispanic neighborhood.

On the table in front of Miss Lucy's picture was a shiny red apple, which Julieta had placed there in remembrance of Miss Lucy's career as a schoolteacher. In front of another picture sat a small plate bearing a slice of the sweet *pan de muerto* – the "bread of the dead" – in remembrance of Julieta's aunt, who loved to bake for family and friends. Likewise, in front of each of the other pictures, there was an appropriately tasteful remembrance.

The table was Julieta's *ofrenda*, or offering, to lure the spirits of the deceased loved ones to visit the two-bedroom home in one of Tucson's oldest neighborhoods. As a further inducement, Julieta decorated the old stucco residence with flowers, including the *cempazuchitl*, a marigold called "the flower of the dead."

Coming the day after the fire at Indigo Bush, the holiday was especially welcome for Julieta, who, as the care home's head administrator, needed something to lift her own spirits.

For Julieta's niece, meanwhile, the holiday provided another opportunity for her to introduce Bryan's nephew to another part of her culture.

"What's with this skeleton candy," Tyler asked Gabriella while visiting her family's home in Tucson's El Rio Neighborhood during the holiday, which fell on a Sunday in 2003. "I thought you said The Day of the Dead is not like Halloween," the third-grader added.

"That candy is called *calaverita* – it's pure sugar in the shape of a skull," said Gabriella. "Halloween is about trick-or-treating and scary costumes and silly stuff like that, but The Day of the Dead is about families visiting cemeteries and about more serious things – and also about everybody having fun with the spirits," added the second-grader (who nearly a year earlier made paper marigolds during the holiday festival at the Tucson Children's Museum).

For Bentley, the holiday was yet another day to enjoy his still relatively new surroundings. He even got to re-enter an old surrounding – the doghouse that Clyde and Callie's parents bought during his brief stay with their family. The sizable shelter – nearly big enough for Bentley to host a canine block party – had finally been relocated to the barrio.

Although Bentley cherished living in a home where he felt safe, he was even more attached to his part-time home. He looked forward to accompanying Indigo Bush's head administrator and its head chef when they went to work. Bentley thought each of the care home's 24 residents was his companion – and the women felt likewise because he gave them unconditional love and one-on-one attention. He listened – and listened – to each of them. He also captivated them with his playful scampering. And he lifted their spirits.

Bentley was especially drawn to Helen. The fact that she discovered him in the care home after his arrival was part of the attraction. Even more so was the fact that she reminded him of another petite, elderly lady – Miss Lucy.

Before Bentley's arrival, Helen had resigned herself to giving up on life. She had refused to undergo badly needed heart surgery. Bentley's appearance, however, changed her outlook. Under Indigo Bush's long-standing policy prohibiting residents from owning pets, Helen could not keep Bentley in her room. Nevertheless, it was common knowledge around Indigo Bush that Helen's room was Bentley's room, too.

Bentley thought the fire was an attack on *his* home. He wanted to confront the fire starter again, but he couldn't know if he would see the burly teenager again. At the moment, he was more concerned about the health of three of his buddies.

The ankle injury that Helen sustained while trying to pick up Bentley before the fire spread near the East Wing's exit door was found to be a mild sprain. And her continuing recuperation from heart surgery was not jeopardized.

As for Daisy, a disinfectant and antibacterial ointment were used for the burns on her thin legs. The Chihuahua's recovery was expected to be speedy.

As for Juanita, she remained unconscious in the hospital's intensive care unit. The smoke inhalation had taken a serious toll on the octogenarian. It was not yet clear whether she would be able to pull through.

One of Julieta's neighbors had suggested Julieta might be able to help Juanita by consulting a *curandera*, a Hispanic healer who administers her treatments by using magic or other unconventional means. Julieta, however, already had decided to go where Juanita would have gone for spiritual assistance.

Next: "The White Dove of the Desert"

Bentley and the Great Fire

A candle lighted by Julieta burns at Mission San Xavier del Bac. Bentley is there only in spirit.

Paw Prints: At the Indigo Bush care home, Bentley became a lifesaver — literally – during the fire, whose starter was seen only by him. One of the residents has been hospitalized for smoke inhalation, and the home's head administrator, Julieta, has decided to make a pilgrimage in behalf of the elderly woman.

Chapter 6 – "The White Dove of the Desert"

Julieta waved goodbye to Bentley, who was whimpering while Bryan held him in his arms near the curb outside their home. The young woman knew how much Bentley enjoyed car rides, but she was on a mission – to a mission.

Specifically, she was driving a few miles south of Tucson to Mission San Xavier del Bac.

The church, whose construction was completed in 1797, had long been regarded as the finest example of Spanish mission architecture in the United States. Its blend of Moorish, Byzantine and Mexican Renaissance styles formed an inspirational landmark in the community of Wa:k in the San Xavier District of the Tohono O'odham Nation. The Indian word "bac" was a reference to the nearby stream. Since the 1950s, however, only rainwater had flowed in the Santa Cruz's otherwise dry riverbed.

Julieta parked in the large expanse of barren desert in front of the whitewashed structure, affectionately called "The White Dove of the Desert." The mostly adobe building, a national landmark, still served as the year-round house of worship for the O'odham, formerly known as the Papago.

Julieta's car was not far from the scaffolding that rose along one of the two 80-foot towers – the one with the dome. (It remained a mystery why the other bell tower was never capped.) The scaffolding was for the restoration project that was being carried out by Patronato San Xavier, the group dedicated to the preservation of the church. The interior, seemingly filled with frescoes and statues, had undergone extensive rejuvenation over a six-year period in the 1990s.

Julieta entered the church through an open mesquite-wood door. The church's interior was shaped like a Latin cross. She walked past rows of pews before pausing amid the crossbeam and standing beneath the 55-foot-high, rounded ceiling, whose artwork was eye-catching. She turned to her left and went into the side chapel that contained the wooden reclining statue of San Francisco Xavier, Juanita's patron saint.

In front of the metal stand bearing vigil lights, Julieta lighted a candle in behalf of the hospitalized woman. While the flame glowed in the tall glass, Julieta sat alone on the bench near the clothed statue that was adorned with small handwritten notes, snapshots, and *milagros* – pinned tokens offered as a form of a wish. Julieta had not brought a button from one of Juanita's blouses or some other such symbol of the Indigo Bush resident. Julieta was content to pray quietly while looking at the candle that she had lighted.

After praying for Juanita's full recovery, Julieta began praying for herself. She asked for guidance and strength to meet a challenge that she could not have foreseen when she was promoted from the job of assistant administrator.

In her first three months after succeeding an unpopular disciplinarian, the graduate of Sunnyside High School and the University of Arizona had succeeded in establishing a family atmosphere at Indigo Bush. The home's residents felt respected, appreciated, and well cared for. They also felt safe.

The shocking fire, however, threatened to undermine Julieta's positive approach as a first-time head administrator. The fact that the blaze was deliberately set dismayed and frightened the care home's residents. Why would someone want to burn down our home? they asked. Who could do such a horrible thing? they also asked.

While remaining seated in the church, Julieta replayed in her mind a short version of the whirlwind of actions she had taken since the fire was discovered by Bentley. There was the evacuation from the home's activity room. There were meetings with Fire Department and Police Department personnel. An emergency meeting of the board of directors of the foundation that oversaw Indigo Bush. Contacts with fire insurance company representatives. Arrangements for damage repairs, some of which required immediate attention. A visit to a hospital room – Juanita's. A follow-up regarding the condition of an ankle injury – Helen's. Let's see . . . what else was there? Oh, yes, how could Julieta forget: There was the meeting she had with the residents. She thought it went well. She was calm, informative, and reassuring. And she was the same way in the meeting she had with Indigo Bush's staff. She did not have an assistant as yet, so she had to be the spearhead on several fronts.

    Wait! There was more, including the series of phone calls she made to representatives of various organizations – the Pima Council on Aging, to name one. Then, there were the . . . no, stop . . . Julieta's recap was boggling her mind.

    The twentysomething woman rose from the bench and slowly walked out of the church. She was on her way to make another visit to the hospital to see Juanita. As she drove away from the old church, she thought about what Juanita had said after Helen first discovered Bentley inside the care home. Juanita said Bentley's presence was *"una bendición y una seña de Dios,"* Julieta recalled, repeating the Spanish words in her mind in English – "a blessing and a sign from God." In view of Bentley's heroic role in the fire, Julieta thought that his presence was indeed a blessing. She did not know what to make of the other part of Juanita's opinion of Bentley.

Julieta planned to stop at Indigo Bush after her hospital visit. Among other things, she wanted to continue making arrangements for a temporary replacement for the care home's fire-wrecked front entryway. During her stop at Indigo Bush, she was to meet up with Bryan and Bentley.

While Julieta drove to the hospital, Bryan drove with Bentley to her thirtysomething brother's nearby El Rio Neighborhood home, on Tucson's West Side, where Bentley would get to play with another visitor – Bryan's young nephew Tyler – and with Julieta's young niece Gabriella, who lived there.

"C'mon! Get it, Bentley," Gabriella said, holding a small beanbag over the Chihuahua's head. "Good boy!" she added after Bentley stood up on his back legs and grabbed the light-blue toy bear with his teeth. His tail was wagging because he enjoyed playing tug of war and because he had heard the name Miss Lucy had given him. She had called him "Boy." Helen had given him the name "Bentley," which was the name of the coffeehouse she saw him running past when he was fleeing the abusive children of the parents who adopted him after Miss Lucy had passed away.

Bentley had forgiven Clyde and Callie, both of whom were on probation and doing community service, as ordered by Pima County Juvenile Court. The twins, who had turned 12 and recently entered the sixth grade, looked forward to having periodic visits with their former companion. Bentley couldn't have known that the first such visit would be coming soon and that the reunion would include another look at a potential killer.

Next: The Moonwalker

Bentley and the Great Fire

Bentley walks on the moon – at least he imagines doing so at the Pima Air & Space Museum.

🐾 *Paw Prints: The identity of the arsonist remains known only to Bentley, who saved the lives of the residents at the care home. While the home's head administrator copes with challenges resulting from the fire, Bentley wonders if he will ever see the arsonist again.* 🐾

Chapter 7 – The Moonwalker

"So it's Bentley who's the one who wants to take a look?" the silver-haired man asked, trying not to chuckle.

"This is his only chance," Callie insisted as she held the watchful Chihuahua in her arms.

"You know we can't bring a dog in there with us when we have the rendezvous with the comet," explained Clyde, who was standing beside his sister near the door to the Challenger Learning Center of the Southwest, located at the Pima Air & Space Museum.

Accompanied by responsible companions, dogs were permitted on the grounds at the mostly outdoor Tucson facility, the largest privately funded aerospace museum in the world with more than 250 aircraft on display.

"Well, I did tell Bryan that you can go inside for a few minutes," the tour guide said, gesturing toward the twentysomething man standing behind the two sixth-graders. In addition to being a volunteer at the museum, the tour guide was a volunteer handyman at Indigo Bush, where he was known as Mr. Fix-it. "Let's go. Follow me."

"Thank you," the 12-year-old twins said in unison, heeding Mr. Fix-it's directions while Bryan tagged along.

"This here is one of the 46 Challenger Learning Centers

in the United States," Mr. Fix-it said, opening the door inside one of the museum's half-dozen buildings. "It was number 32 when it opened in March 1999. These centers came about in remembrance of the crew of the Challenger space shuttle."

"That's the one that had the crash in 1986 with the teacher in the crew," Clyde said, recalling a school assignment. "Christa McAuliffe is her name," he added.

"That's correct," Mr. Fix-it said, stopping after taking several steps into what looked like a long, wide hallway. "It's quiet in here now, but it won't be when you kids go on your mission with your classmates. You will see lights flashing. You will hear … well, don't let me spoil it for you now," he added, biting his tongue while standing in the section that served as the launch pad. "Let's just say you'll really get an idea of what it's like to be rocketed into space."

"I can't wait!" cried Callie, her voice momentarily drawing Bentley's attention away from the black door.

"After your shuttle is in orbit," continued the aviation-combat veteran of World War II, "you'll pass through this airlock." He proceeded to lead Bentley, the two youngsters and Bryan through the adjacent revolving door, which reminded Bryan of the door to a photographer's darkroom.

The black door opened into a much larger area, which served as the space station laboratory. In there, Clyde and Callie and their classmates would conduct experiments and send a space probe to meet the comet.

"There are going to be some surprises in store for them on their mission," Mr. Fix-it said, gesturing toward the twins while grinning at Bryan.

"I can imagine," Bryan said, returning the grin.

"You mean like emergencies and stuff?" Clyde asked, gawking at the numerous computer consoles under the low lighting in the wide room. "We've found out that there's – "

"You'll find out that learning is fun," Mr. Fix-it said, cutting off any discussion that might reveal any of the secrets awaiting the skinny, little twins and their classmates. "Now follow me," the lanky man added, proceeding to lead the tour group into the mock-up of the national space agency's Mission Control room in Houston. "This room is where the communications with the shuttle crew will be maintained. This is where you'll see how important teamwork is."

"Could we get a couple of pictures of Bentley in this room?" Clyde asked, raising his disposable camera with his right hand. "Just Bentley. Real quick. We promise."

"OK, but make it fast," Mr. Fix-it said. "The museum is closing for the day."

"Cal, can you hold Bentley in front of those patches?" Clyde asked, gesturing toward the wall with the insignias from NASA shuttle missions.

In Callie's arms, Bentley poses for Clyde amid the insignias from NASA shuttle missions.

After Callie positioned Bentley for the photograph, she cooperated with her brother for one more shot. The second was of Bentley in front of another wall. The backdrop this time was out of this world: It was a panoramic view of the mostly bluish planet Earth as seen from the powdery-white landscape of the moon. Bentley appeared to be an adventurous moonwalker, seemingly climbing lunar rocks.

A few moments later, Mr. Fix-it announced that the preview was over, and he escorted the tour group from the Challenger Learning Center. Callie then handed Bentley back to Bryan.

After saying goodbye to Mr. Fix-it, Clyde and Callie rejoined their parents, who were waiting outdoors. The young couple had run into three acquaintances from their real estate business and ended up in a lengthy discussion, even though they would have preferred to accompany their children on the brief tour before the family's visit to the museum concluded.

The museum visit was Bryan's idea. Indigo Bush's head chef had promised that the family could have reunions with Bentley after he and his wife Julieta – the care home's head administrator – became Bentley's companions. The family's visit to the museum was the first time Clyde and Callie had seen Bentley in more than three months – since eight days after their abusive behavior toward him led him to escape from the family's home.

Bryan thanked Indigo Bush's volunteer handyman for giving Clyde and Callie a preview of the twins' interactive science adventure. He then carried Bentley outdoors and set him down on the ground. Bentley, leashed, began walking with Bryan and his former companions to the parking lot.

During the walk, Bryan received a call on his cell phone. It was from the hospital: Juanita had finally regained consciousness and was expected to fully recover from the smoke inhalation she suffered one week earlier in the fire at the care home. Clyde, who dreamed of becoming a firefighter someday, was especially delighted to hear the good news.

In the parking lot, Bryan said goodbye to Clyde and Callie and their parents, and he gave them a few moments to say goodbye to Bentley before he lifted Bentley onto the passenger seat of the pickup truck.

Bryan began driving out of the parking lot. Suddenly, Bentley began barking, drawing the attention of the young pedestrian nearby.

"Easy. Calm down," Bryan said in a soothing voice, his eyes focused on his restless passenger.

Bentley kept barking until he could no longer see the person who was walking in the parking lot. Bentley had seen him before – holding a gas can. The pedestrian was the burly teenager who started the fire at Bentley's part-time home.

Next: The Cabin in the Woods

Bentley walks near the cabin in the White Mountains.

🐾 *Paw Prints: Two weeks have gone by since the fire at the care home. The resident who suffered smoke inhalation has regained consciousness and begun showing further improvement. The arsonist remains at large, his identity known only to Bentley, who had seen him again a week ago walking in a parking lot.* 🐾

Chapter 8 – The Cabin in the Woods

BENTLEY AND THE GREAT FIRE / CH. 8 – THE CABIN IN THE WOODS

    Bentley had not felt such a chill on such a sunny day before, but he had not been so far from his hometown before, either. He was taking a morning walk in Arizona's White Mountains, about 200 miles northeast of Tucson. He was a guest at a cabin owned by Bryan's grandparents.
    The cabin in the woods was near Show Low, which was founded in 1870 and whose name came from a legendary card game in which the winner turned up the deuce of clubs.
    Bentley was spending the second weekend before Thanksgiving at the mini-chateau-style structure built in 1983 with pine logs on property at an altitude over a mile high – 6,300 feet. He was staying with Grandpa Grant and Grandma Doris, who were asleep in the bedroom on the ground floor, and with four other people, including Bryan, who was with him on his walk amid the juniper trees and ponderosa pines.
    In the cabin's spacious loft, a large bed rested between two small ones. The middle bed was shared by Bryan, his wife Julieta and their four-footed companion. Assigned to sleep to their right was Julieta's niece Gabriella, and stationed on their left was Bryan's nephew Tyler.
    Soon after escorting Bentley back inside the cabin, Bryan learned that all the sleepyheads had woke up and were looking forward to a big breakfast. Indigo Bush's head chef,

who was known for his resourcefulness and inventiveness, then went to the kitchen and prepared his belly-buster – Southwestern scrambled eggs, home fried potatoes, sausage patties, bacon strips, buttermilk pancakes, homemade biscuits and gravy, and, oh yes, peanut butter French toast. He also served up fresh fruit, jellies, orange juice, coffee and milk.

    The menu was far more extensive than what Bryan could ever prepare at Indigo Bush in light of the care home's limited financial means. At the cabin, however, Bryan's generous grandfather had urged him to be generous in the kitchen. Bryan, who was a Tucson High Magnet School graduate and who was taking business classes at night at Pima Community College in hopes of opening his own restaurant someday, appreciated the opportunity.

    Bryan was already mentally preparing an early dinner when Grandpa Grant again told him how his carrying the two residents out of the care home during the fire had made Bryan an even greater source of pride in their family, as well as in the Tucson community at large. Bryan once again downplayed his heroism and gave credit to Bentley for alerting him. (About five months later, Bryan would be among the honorees at the annual American Red Cross Southern Arizona Chapter's Real Heroes Breakfast.)

Bentley and the Great Fire / Ch. 8 – The Cabin in the Woods

With the weather warming up late in the morning, Gabriella and Tyler took Bentley along on their hunting trip. A short distance from the cabin, the young hunters with the jackets and jeans found their prey – a pine cone. Then, they quickly found another cone and another. Soon, they were filling their plastic sacks with cones of all shapes and sizes.

"Wait 'til your mom and dad see all of these," Gabriella told Tyler. "They'll have enough pine cones to light the logs in your home's fireplace for a million years," the second-grader added excitedly.

"I promised them I'd bring back some cones, but I didn't expect to fill my uncle's truck with 'em," Tyler said, topping off another white sack. "Maybe there won't be enough room left for us to ride back to Tucson with the cones and we'll have to stay here a while – until it starts to snow," the third-grader added, laughing.

"That would be fun," Gabriella said, joining in on the laughter. "I'd like to make a snowball for once in my life."

"We should ask Bentley to help us build a snowman," Tyler joked.

"I have no idea how he'd be with snow, but we could find out," Gabriella said, grinning. "What do you think about that, Bentley?"

Ch. 8 – The Cabin in the Woods

Bentley, of course, was a good listener – one who appreciated a good joke. Being only 2 years old and a Tucsonan, he had never set a paw in snow. Nevertheless, he had heard about snow in the stories that Miss Lucy had read to him. He had seen snow in the photographs that she had shown him. And he had even watched snow falling during each of the winters of his life when he and his first companion sat in front of her TV for the network broadcast of her favorite Christmas movie, "It's a Wonderful Life."

Bentley loved children, and he thought children loved snow. So he thought he would help build the snowman.

The snowman, however, would have to cool his heels. Their tall sacks overflowing with cones, Gabriella and Tyler called off the hunt. Their decision proved timely. Once back indoors, they were invited to go on a road trip with Bryan and Julieta. Bentley, of course, would come along for the ride. The drive toward the nearly Pinetop-Lakeside area ended in the parking area at the Mogollon Rim Overlook, named after the governor in the early 1700s of what was then Spanish territory. The riders became hikers and followed the Nature Trail as it meandered amid the towering pines. They stopped when they reached the sandstone rock outcrop. From there, they had a scenic view of the tree-studded valley below a portion of the Mogollon Rim, a slope ranging from 1,000 to 2,000 feet from its base to its highest plateau. The 200-mile-long row of cliffs in north-central Arizona was the dividing line between the pine forests in the higher elevations of the state's northern region and the cactus vegetation in the lowland deserts to the south.

Gazing at the autumn colors of the trees, Julieta felt grateful for the soothing sight and said a quiet prayer of thankfulness. Indigo Bush's head administrator also felt grateful that her plea at the church for Juanita's recovery from smoke inhalation had been granted. And she felt grateful that the care home's residents were coping as well as could be expected with the damage to the old building.

At that moment, Julieta was able to see the forest for the trees – figuratively speaking. She realized what was needed for the care home. Yet again, she was grateful.

Bentley, meanwhile, wondered what more he could do to single out the person who started the fire. He remembered that his barking upon seeing the arsonist again had failed to draw other people's attention to the burly teenager. He continued to look at the colorful valley, but he was not able to see the forest for the trees – at least not yet.

Next: "The Gentleman Caller"

In a snapshot taken by Helen, Bentley is held by her friend Ruth outside the Fox Theatre in Tucson.

Paw Prints: Three weeks have gone by since the fire at the care home. While on a visit to the White Mountains, Indigo Bush's head administrator came up with an idea for the home's future. During the same visit, Bentley was unable to figure out what more he could do to single out the arsonist, whose identity he alone knew.

Chapter 9 – "The Gentleman Caller"

Bentley and the Great Fire / Ch. 9 – "The Gentleman Caller"

"Round and round he goes and where he stops, no one knows," Helen told Ruth as they watched Bentley walk in circles before lying down between them on the sofa at the Indigo Bush Assisted Living and Residential Care Home.

"Why does he turn so much?" Ruth asked her friend.

"I don't know exactly," Helen said, shaking her head. "It has something to do with instinct," she added, gently patting the Chihuahua on his back while being mindful of the genetic hip problem that restricted his jumping.

There were many theories about the many things that pets did, Miss Lucy had pointed out. In one theory, circling was a nesting behavior that could be traced back to their ancestral need in the wild to trample high grass to create a bed before lying down, Bentley's first companion had read.

"A few of the platinum girls are saying the fire investigators must be going around in circles," Ruth said, using her affectionate term for the care home's residents. "I think those ladies are being unrealistic in expecting to have the case solved already," added the heavyset woman, who was one of the two advocates for the two dozen residents.

"I know these things take time," Helen said. "It is frustrating, though, when we don't hear of any breakthrough of any sort," added the thin woman, sighing.

Helen's frustration was shared by Julieta, who was sitting at her desk in Indigo Bush's administrative office. The head administrator had been in frequent contact with the authorities, but had only heard of things being ruled out. Still, she was heartened by the many sympathetic calls and letters the care home had received from the public. And she remained hopeful that someone would phone the Pima County Attorney's Office's 88-CRIME hotline or some other agency and provide information leading to an arrest.

In the meantime, Julieta expected, the authorities would continue looking into the lives of Indigo Bush's residents and staffers to see if there were any reasons why someone from outside the care home would try to harm anyone in the home.

The only sign of violence that Julieta could recall since around the time she became head administrator came when Abigail revealed what her ex-boyfriend had done to her. The teenage volunteer's arms were battered, but she had worn long-sleeved tops to conceal the abuse. Julieta had told the fire investigators about the ex-boyfriend's behavior, for which he was being punished through Pima County Juvenile Court. The investigators, however, later told Julieta that the burly teenager was not a suspect because he had a good alibi.

Although keeping track of the investigation was a priority for Julieta, she managed to return her attention to another priority – planning for Indigo Bush's future. She was using the weekend before Thanksgiving to finish preparing for her meeting with the board of directors of the foundation that oversaw the care home. She intended to tell the board about the revelation she experienced while standing on an outcrop along the Mogollon Rim in the White Mountains.

While Julieta continued to outline her idea on notebook paper at her desk, a visitor came into Indigo Bush's temporary entrance and nearly ran into Abigail.

"Excuse me," he said after startling the pretty teenager.

"What are you doing in here?" the high school junior asked him. "Aren't you off today?"

"Oh, I'm not here on business," the silver-haired man said, grinning. "Today I'm what's known as 'the gentleman caller,' " added Indigo Bush's volunteer handyman.

Realizing that Mr. Fix-it was wearing a white shirt and navy-blue pants, instead of his usual gray work clothes, Abigail began smiling. "You mean you're finally going to call on her, don't you," the 17-year-old volunteer said, her smile widening.

"We've known each other since she moved here almost two years ago," Mr. Fix-it said, nodding his head. "We're not getting any younger."

"You'll always be young at heart," the red-haired teenager protested. "Well, don't let me keep you any longer from doing your calling," she added, stepping away from the lanky gentleman. "Good luck, though I don't think you'll need it."

"Thank you," Mr. Fix-it said, sighing. "I can use all the luck I can get," he added while walking in the opposite direction.

Mr. Fix-it went to the East Wing and saw Bentley entering the room that was full of saguaro cactus images, including those dotting the Western-themed wall mural.

When Mr. Fix-it reached the open doorway, he saw Bentley resting in the arms of the woman who was standing in the middle of the room.

"Hello," Helen said upon realizing there was a visitor at her door. "What can I do for you?" she added cheerfully.

"You can say 'yes' to the question I'm about to ask you," the hazel-eyed man said somewhat nervously.

"What question?" Helen asked, stepping toward him.

"Will you go out to dinner with me?" Mr. Fix-it asked, trying his best to make it sound like an invitation, rather than a plea.

"Yes," Helen said, surprising him. "Maybe in a few months from now . . . when my recovery is further along."

"It's a date then," Mr. Fix-it said, taking a step forward.

"No more dating for me, not at this time in my life," the seventysomething widow said quietly.

"If it's not a date, what do we call it?" the eightysomething widower asked, sounding and looking puzzled.

"A get-together," Helen replied. "Let's just call it that."

"Well, how about dinner *and* a movie someday?" Mr. Fix countered. "I mean someday after our get-"

"A movie? I haven't been to a movie in I don't know how long. What movie are you talking about?"

"A Fred Astaire and Ginger Rogers movie? Whatever's playing downtown at the Fox Theatre when it reopens, whenever that is," Mr. Fix-it said. "We talked about going there many years ago with our spouses, remember?"

"It was quite a palace in its heyday," the retired photographer said of the Fox, a unique blend of Southwestern and Art Deco architectural styles and one of only nine movie houses designated a national landmark. "It was built in 1929, you know. I took some shots of the re-created FOX sign they put up in 2002; I even have Bentley in one of them. I'm glad there's that restoration group around to give it a new lease on life," she added, referring to the Fox Tucson Theatre Foundation.

"We could all use a new lease on life," Mr. Fix-it said, laughing.

"Tell me about it," Helen said, joining in the laughter. "Heart surgery does wonders," added the woman who suddenly thought Bentley was lighter than a feather.

For the moment, Bentley was content to put off his concerns about the arsonist and snuggle in her loving arms.

Next: Giving Thanks

Bentley and the Great Fire

Bentley joins the Thanksgiving celebration at the Indigo Bush care home.

🐾 *Paw Prints: Twenty-six days have gone by since the fire at the care home. A few of the residents have said they think the investigators must be going around in circles. The home's head administrator has been asking for patience. The fire starter's identity remains known only to Bentley.* 🐾

Chapter 10 – Giving Thanks

"And last, but not least, we are thankful for Bentley, the little guy who has made such a big difference in our lives," Pastor Connie added as she finished saying grace at the Thanksgiving meal in the Indigo Bush care home.

"*Si, mi compañero pequeño*," Juanita called out to Pastor Connie, who was standing under the archway between the two small dining rooms.

"Yes, he's a 'little buddy' to each of us," the woman wearing the clerical collar replied, prompting other diners to say, "Amen."

"Bon appétit!" said Bryan, who was standing directly across from Pastor Connie. "Happy Thanksgiving, ladies," added the man wearing the white uniform. The care home's head chef had prepared a traditional turkey dinner with all the fixings, including several high-quality donations from the Salvage Program at the Community Food Bank.

"Everybody start eating," urged Julieta, who was standing next to Bryan. The home's head administrator then gestured for Pastor Connie to join her at the nearby table. While the 26 diners got down to business, Bentley and Daisy were taking an afternoon nap in Julieta's office on the dog bed that was spread on the floor. The canine pals had plenty of room to stretch out on the round, plaid cushion, which was 3 feet across.

 Back in the kitchen, Bryan made sure the dinner went as planned, and he set aside two small paper plates of cut-up turkey meat to feed to the two Chihuahuas later.

 Over dinner, Julieta thanked Pastor Connie for having said a prayer that her meeting with the board of directors would go well. At the meeting, which was held three days earlier, Julieta presented her vision for Indigo Bush's future.

 "Of course, I didn't tell the board that it came to me *in* a vision," Julieta said between bites of moist turkey. "It wasn't a vision, but it was like a vision. You know what I mean."

 "Yes, like you said the last time we talked, you were in the White Mountains for the weekend, and it suddenly came to you," Pastor Connie said between bites of candied yams.

 When Julieta was looking at the valley below the Mogollon Rim during her weekend getaway, Julieta thought of the large patch of prickly pear cactus plants that stretched across the back of the parking lot behind the care home. She envisioned the vegetation replaced by a one-story, multi-winged structure housing the new Indigo Bush Assisted Living and Residential Care Home. The white stucco complex had numerous windows and a large courtyard, and its look was modern but with the architectural influence of the old Southwest – at least that was how her mind's eye saw it.

In subsequent gatherings back in Tucson with Indigo Bush's residents and her staff, Julieta outlined her vision and heard their viewpoints.

During the lengthy meeting with the directors of the board of the foundation that oversaw Indigo Bush, Julieta noted that the damage to the care home would be repaired with the fire insurance money, but that the home would remain a mostly outdated structure. The old building, which was originally a sanitarium for tuberculosis patients, had been extensively "grandfathered," or exempted from certain regulations for buildings in the city of Tucson.

Julieta envisioned a new care home in full compliance with all the regulations – and with rooms for twice as many residents, including men.

"Rooms for men, too?" Pastor Connie asked, setting her fork down.

"Our home's ladies told me that it's fine with them," Julieta said. "It's also fine with the board. In fact, the board likes the whole plan," she added, smiling. "Most of it had been in the back of my mind for years – and in the back of the minds of the directors. I happened to be in the right place at the right time. And I had you praying for me."

"The power of prayer can never be underestimated," Pastor Connie said, winking her right eye.

"Of course, the directors will continue to provide their input, and we'll have to consider our options," Julieta said. "For example, half of the new home could be built on the land in back. Then, the residents in this old building could be relocated there. Then, this building could be demolished and replaced with the other half of the new home."

"But?" asked Pastor Connie. "There is always a 'but,' am I right?"

"It's the money, as you can imagine," Julieta said, frowning. "The foundation owns the land, so that's not the problem. But the cost of building the new home would be tremendous. On the other hand, the project would have to be built on this large a scale to cover our costs down the road."

"It's sort of a Catch-22, isn't it?" asked Pastor Connie. "You can't afford to build big, but you can't afford not to."

"Exactly," Julieta said, sighing. "Unless . . ."

"Unless what?" Pastor Connie asked.

"Unless we win the Powerball jackpot," Julieta said, only half-joking. "Can you say a prayer for that?"

"What do you say we give thanks for the board's positive response, and we'll see how things go from there?" Pastor Connie said, picking up her fork again.

"That sounds fair enough," Julieta said before resuming her Thanksgiving dining.

While Julieta and Pastor Connie were giving thanks for the board's receptiveness, other people at Indigo Bush were giving thanks for various other reasons.

Helen, for example, was thankful that she was alive and doing fairly well after her heart surgery, and that, figuratively speaking, her heart was no longer closed to a romantic overture, such as Mr. Fix-it's dinner-and-a-movie invitation.

Helen's friend Ruth was thankful that the Southern Arizona Chapter of the Arthritis Foundation helped her cope with her mobility problem, and that, among other things, so many University of Arizona Wildcat sporting events were televised (by the way, she kept a 1997 national men's basketball championship T-shirt in her room).

Juanita was thankful that she had the strength – both physical and spiritual – to survive the fire, and that, among other things, her friend Maria volunteered to let her move in while Juanita's room was getting repaired.

Bryan was thankful that the ladies enjoyed his Thanksgiving cooking (ever inventive, he had put Craisins in the turkey dressing for the first time), and that, among other things, he had two well-behaved Chihuahuas at feeding time.

Bentley and Daisy were thankful for the tasty treat.

Bentley was also thankful that Miss Lucy had been his first companion and that she had read to him about the need for giving thanks.

Next: Playtime

BENTLEY AND THE GREAT FIRE

Bentley retrieves the fabric rope thrown by Tyler during a game of fetch outside the boy's house.

🐾 *Paw Prints: Six weeks have gone by since the fire at the care home. The repair work has been progressing. The proposal for replacing the old home with a new home has been well received, but its approval has been made conditional on finding a major financial donor. The arson investigation, meanwhile, has not been progressing. The arsonist's identity still remains known only to Bentley.* 🐾

Chapter 11 – Playtime

It was 12 days before Christmas, and all through the house, Bentley could be heard scurrying about.

At the moment, the black-and-tan Chihuahua was in the garage. He stuck his head between two plastic sacks filled with pine cones and grabbed the fabric bone with his teeth. Then, he returned the knotted rope to his playmates.

Gabriella and Tyler were taking turns throwing the 10-inch-long toy and watching Bentley retrieve it.

Playing fetch was one of Bentley's favorite games. The uncertainty as to which direction he would have to run was one of the game's attractions for him.

Not all dogs play fetch, Miss Lucy had pointed out. But those who do play have the opportunity to exercise their muscles, reduce their stress and have fun, Bentley's first companion had read.

Bentley loved playtime. The game itself was what most interested him, not the location. He enjoyed playing at his home with his companions Julieta and Bryan, at his part-time home with the residents of the Indigo Bush care home, and at homes in which he was a guest.

At the moment, he was a guest in the home owned by Tyler's parents, Lola and Tony. The thirtysomething couple lived on Tucson's Southeast Side in Rita Ranch, one of the area's newer developments. Lola was Bryan's older sister.

Gabriella and Tyler – the flower girl and the ring bearer at Julieta and Bryan's wedding – had become such good friends that their parents knew all about commuting by car between Rita Ranch and Tucson's El Rio Neighborhood, where Gabriella lived.

"You're so cool, Bentley," Tyler said as the fetcher dropped the multicolored rope on the concrete landing near the garage doorway. "Now we're going to see how you do when you really get room to run," he added, picking up the toy by one of its frayed ends.

"Where are you going?" Gabriella asked Tyler as he walked into the adjacent hallway.

"Follow me," Tyler told her. "You, too, Bentley."

Bentley sprinted after Tyler – and the fabric rope. Soon Bentley was in the home's back yard with his two playmates.

"OK, Bentley," Tyler said, waving the rope to draw Bentley's full attention. "Here goes!" he yelled, throwing the toy as far as he could.

Bentley ran across the wide yard and found the rope resting a few feet from a tall, skinny cactus. The smooth cactus was one of the numerous plants in the yard owned by

Lola and Tony, who were the operators of an East Side garden nursery.

The angled plant, which was near a colorful mosaic-tile table designed by a Tucson artist, was a cereus cactus. It was about 6 feet tall and no more than 5 inches wide. Much to Tyler's surprise, the cactus produced 6-inch-wide, white flowers.

Bentley grabbed the rope with his mouth and raced back to his playmates.

"He's so fast," Gabriella told Tyler. "He can do so many things. We don't know half of them."

The young girl was correct, of course.

Bentley's talents were indeed impressive, Miss Lucy had pointed out. In addition to his lightning speed and numerous other athletic skills, he was highly intelligent, warmly affectionate and, among other things, a reliable smile-inducer, she had said.

Bentley's enthusiasm for life had proved to be therapeutic for the residents of his part-time home. The Indigo Bush ladies couldn't help but be energized by his tail-wagging cheerfulness. Helen, for example, had resumed taking photographs and was no longer resigned to abandoning her social life.

Helen's friend Ruth continued to show progress while coping with her arthritis. She also had coaxed Helen and two other residents – Xenia and Vivien – to join her in her room to watch telecasts of University of Arizona basketball games.

Indigo Bush's staff and its volunteers were likewise energized by Bentley. Mr. Fix-it, for example, had been so motivated that he finally voiced his fondness for Helen by asking her out on a date – or, as she put it, a get-together.

The unconditional love that Bentley gave Indigo Bush's residents had even swayed one resident who was thought by some to be a lost cause. Josephine, a retired civil rights advocate, was finally dealing with her periodic memory lapses with the help of the Desert Southwest Chapter of the Alzheimer's Association. She also was demonstrating her renewed community interest by making a financial contribution to the Dunbar Coalition, which was working to convert the building that housed her old segregated school into an African-American museum and cultural center.

Bentley's nearly fatal encounter more than four months ago with the coyote and his subsequent dreamlike visit to Rainbow Bridge had made him understand that his mission was to fulfill his ancestral role and serve the elderly ladies. The Aztec Indians used his ancestors as guides for the spirits of the dead, Miss Lucy had read to him. Chihuahuas were bridges between this life and the next, she had believed.

Bentley knew he could be of further service by identifying the young person who started the fire at Indigo Bush. He had seen the burly teenager again, five weeks ago in the parking lot at the Pima Air & Space Museum. Bentley was patiently awaiting the next sighting, during which he was determined to make the arsonist's presence known to other people.

In the meantime, Bentley was content to bide his time and enjoy his playtime with the new member of the Tucson Arizona Boys Chorus and the new member of the Ballet Folklórico San Juan. He could not have known that he soon would have another potentially dangerous encounter with the fire starter.

Next: A Small Patch of Red Sky

Bentley sits quietly in the pickup truck after the driver abducted him and the teenager who was walking him.

> 🐾 *Paw Prints: Seven weeks have gone by since the fire at the care home. The arsonist's identity remains known only to Bentley, who has been waiting to see the burly teenager again and make the youth's presence known to other people.* 🐾

Chapter 12 – A Small Patch of Red Sky

Bentley and the Great Fire / Ch. 12 - A Small Patch of Red Sky

The wind was stronger than what Bentley liked, but Bentley liked walking with Abigail. That would explain why he was braving the brisk breeze near the street corner a few blocks from his part-time home five days before Christmas.

Or, as Lara, a resident at the Indigo Bush care home, would put it, the first full day of Hanukkah, the eight-day-long celebration of the Jewish "Festival of Light."

Abigail had made a habit of walking Bentley with his leash each Saturday afternoon when the volunteer helped out at the home. The red-haired teenager always took the same route. The normally quiet corner marked the halfway point.

"All right, it's time for us to head back again," said the high school junior wearing the green jacket and tan pants.

While slowly retracting the black leash's nylon lead, Abigail heard Bentley growling, and then the engine roaring. A second or two later, she heard Bentley barking, and then the tires screeching, which muffled the opening of the doors.

Before she finished turning around, Abigail was grabbed at the waist by the burly teenager. "I need you to take a ride with me," the former football player said firmly as he held onto her while she held onto the leash's casing.

"Zack! Let go of me!" Abigail told her ex-boyfriend. "You're under a court order not to come anywhere near me!"

"Don't worry," Zack said, shuffling Abigail toward his massive pickup truck. "I swear I'm not going to hurt you."

Bentley yelped, and Abigail realized the leash's 16-foot-long cord was twisted. "Stop pushing me, and let me get the dog's leash untangled," she said as calmly as she could.

"I don't have time for all this," Zack grumbled, freeing his right hand and untangling the leash. "Give me this," he added, grabbing the leash's casing. "He's coming with us."

"Don't you dare hurt him!" Abigail warned the former offensive lineman with the spiky black hair and the long-sleeved, plaid shirt and black jeans.

"Ladies first," Zack said, hoisting Abigail onto the passenger seat. "Now for the other one," he added, turning in time to catch the lunging Chihuahua by the shoulders. "In you go, leash and all!" he added before shutting the door.

Bentley barked, then quickly quieted down after he was lifted onto the seat below the sliding glass window in the truck's extended cab. He looked upward at the other stunned passenger, and then at the speeding driver.

Although the burly teenager had grabbed him, Bentley no longer sensed that the youth intended to harm him. Abigail looked at the back seat and saw that Bentley was alert and uninjured. She then returned her attention to the high school dropout behind the wheel. "Why are you doing this?" she asked. "We're never going to get together again."

"This isn't about that," Zack said, shaking his head. "It's about me having to explain something – that's all."

"I have no idea what you're talking about," Abigail said. "I don't even know where we're going."

"We're going to a place where we've gone before," Zack said, cutting the corner on a right turn. "The old park."

"Whatever," Abigail said, shrugging. "Just remember, after you're done with your explaining, you're driving the dog and me back to where you picked us up."

"That's what I was planning to do all along," Zack said, sounding like he meant it.

After a few minutes of silence, the two 17-year-olds – and Bentley – arrived at the small field. Zack parked the white truck along the row of tall mesquite trees and turned off the engine. "I'm just going to say it," he muttered as he stared at the steering wheel.

"What did you say?" Abigail asked, leaning toward him.

"I'm the one who started that fire, and I did it because I wanted to get back at you for turning me in on the beatings I gave you," Zack blurted out. "There, I said it," he added, sighing. "I'm going to the police after I drive you back."

Abigail slowly leaned away from him. She stared at nothing in particular on the dashboard. She was speechless.

"I know what you're thinking," Zack said after a few seconds. "I know you've probably suspected it was me all along. Well, the police have been on to me, too. And it's like I knew what I did with the fire was bad, but I was only trying to scare you, not hurt you. And . . . well . . . I was doing drugs again at the time, and I didn't know what I was doing."

Abigail continued to stare at the dashboard in silence.

Zack did not mind whether Abigail spoke or not. He resumed his rambling explanation, finally revealing that his father had accidentally discovered that his alibi was false. "I wasn't working at one of his houses like I made him think I was," he said, continuing to stare at the steering wheel. "But I was at one of his houses today, and he told me that his lawyers could help me out again – like they did with the probation I got for hitting you – if I turned myself in."

"Look at that," Abigail murmured, breaking her long silence after lifting her eyes from the dashboard.

"What?" Zack said, lifting his eyes from the wheel.

"See that up there, not far from here?" Abigail asked, pointing with her right forefinger.

"It can't be!" gasped Zack. "Don't tell me it's from that cigarette!"

What Zack and Abigail were looking at was a small patch of red sky along with a column of black smoke. The sight was a result of the fire that Zack unknowingly set at the partially built house in which he and his father had talked. Zack's father had left the construction site, but Zack had lingered to smoke a cigarette. After Zack mindlessly flung his half-smoked cigarette and left, the wood-frame structure became the fire's fuel. With the help of the day's strong wind, the flames jumped to another house under construction, and yet another.

Alerted by passers-by, firefighters prevented the blaze from spreading further and becoming great in scope.

Zack would have more explaining to do.

Abigail was still in a state of shock when she was returned to the normally quiet street corner a few blocks from Indigo Bush. Zack opened the sliding glass window, and Bentley climbed onto the ice chest on the back seat and

BENTLEY AND THE GREAT FIRE / CH. 12 - A SMALL PATCH OF RED SKY

went through the opening onto the pickup truck's bed. Zack took Bentley's leash, lifted him and handed him to Abigail. She quietly resumed walking with Bentley back to the care home, where she would do some explaining of her own.

Bentley emerges from the white pickup truck after Zack returned him and Abigail to where he had seized them.

Bentley instinctively knew the burly teenager was surrendering. But he also knew his part-time home still faced what head administrator Julieta had called "a difficult challenge." And he knew he would have to help her meet that challenge somehow.

Next: The Fire Within

The Green Dragon materializes in Bentley's imagination after he hears about him.

🐾 *Paw Prints: After forcing Bentley and Abigail to ride with him in his truck, Abigail's ex-boyfriend Zack admitted to the Indigo Bush volunteer that he set the fire at the home. Before confronting her, he accidentally started another fire, which burned three houses under construction. On his way to surrendering to the police, he returned Abigail and Bentley to the corner where he abducted them.* 🐾

Chapter 13 – The Fire Within

Bentley and the Great Fire / Ch. 13 - The Fire Within

Three days before Christmas, Indigo Bush's part-time resident was spending another night with Helen, who had left her door ajar intentionally.

During his periodic sleepovers at the home, Bentley would wake up during the night and visit two or three restless residents who had kept their doors open for him.

Some of the elderly ladies would tell Bentley about the good and not-so-good things that had happened to them in their lives. Some would quietly read while he sat with them. And some would be content to simply watch him after he curled up in their laps.

Josephine, who was slumped in her chair, perked up when she saw Bentley. She chuckled after she told herself that now she could forget about her short-term memory lapses, at least for the short term. Bentley's arrival was her cue for yet another recollection about her old school.

The African-American woman, who was a member of the last class to graduate at the Dunbar School in 1951, remained proud of the school named for nationally renowned black poet Paul Laurence Dunbar. The elementary and junior high school had to cope with inferior supplies at times and had encountered other limitations during its 33 years of segregation. Nevertheless, Josephine's determination to learn was unlimited, she recalled. Other members of her class were similarly dedicated, as were their teachers, she also recalled.

In the fall of 1951, the Dunbar building was reopened as the integrated John A. Spring Junior High, named after an early teacher in the Tucson public school system. The Spring school was closed in 1978.

Josephine had been pleased to hear about the continuing effort to convert the historic Dunbar building into an African-American museum and cultural center. The effort was being made by the Dunbar Coalition, consisting of the Dunbar Alumni Association, the Dunbar/Spring Neighborhood Association, the Juneteenth Festival Committee, and the Tucson Urban League (for which Josephine had served as a civil rights advocate before her retirement).

After Josephine began to doze off, Bentley quietly left her and entered the room of the retired interior decorator. Lara, as she called herself, was a member of the Jewish Family & Children's Service of Southern Arizona's Holocaust Survivor Group.

"I look forward, but I don't forget the past," the white-haired, frail woman said a few moments after Bentley sat beside her chair. "I was born in 1930 in Hungary. I lived with my parents and brother in Budapest. But then Hitler's Nazis took over, and we lost our home. 'Take one suitcase,' the Nazis told us when we were assigned to the ghetto. Seven families living there under one roof. Later during World War II, we were herded into cattle cars and taken on the train to the concentration camp. I was separated from my parents and brother, and I never saw them again. I learned they had died in Poland in the gas chambers at Auschwitz.

"I also was taken to the Auschwitz camp, where the air was gray from the ashes and there was the awful smell from the ovens. I was beaten and starved and I was sick with typhus, but I was fortunate to be liberated by the Allied soldiers. I was skin and bones – a teenager weighing 65 pounds – but I was determined to survive. Now I tell all who listen to me to take hatred out of their lives. Over 6 million Jews died in the Holocaust. We, the survivors, continue to speak for them, and we say, 'Never again!' "

After Lara stopped talking and fell asleep, Bentley entered Mei-Li's room, where he had twice before been a guest. He sat on the cushioned footstool in front of her chair. The 100-year-old woman would tell him stories. Not ones about her brutally harsh years in the 1930s in war-torn China (where she had lost her family), nor ones about her many prosperous years later in America as a grocery-store operator in Tucson. Rather, stories about fantastic creatures.

In America and elsewhere in the Western world, noted Mei-Li, dragons were fire-breathing monsters so evil that good humans had to go to heroic lengths to slay them.

However, in Asia, noted Mei-Li, dragons were mist-breathing beings so good that all humans were beholden to them for bestowing rainfall and other beneficial gifts.

In Mei-Li's native land, the Green Dragon was associated with good fortune, wisdom, and generosity, as well as longevity (Mei-Li credited her antique jade dragon pendant with helping her reach the century mark).

Ever the attentive listener, Bentley heard what Mei-Li had to say about how the Green Dragon got his strength.

"There was no fire from his breath," she said in her raspy voice. "He breathed out vapor that changed into clouds. He was so powerful he could bring floods. He could change the flow of the river. He could control the tide. And he drew his strength from the great fire within him.

"In each of us, there is the great fire," Mei-Li continued. "The fire can be good or bad, depending on how it is used. Good can be for energy, courage, love – like you show," she added, patting Bentley's head with her right hand.

"Bad can be for anger, hatred, acting reckless – like the boy who started the fire here has shown. We must be wise like the Green Dragon. We must use the fire within us for good."

After Mei-Li finished speaking and dozed off, Bentley returned to Helen's room and curled up alongside the woman asleep in the bed. He closed his eyes, but he wasn't ready to sleep. Instead, he kept thinking about what he had just heard.

The fire at the care home had directly threatened the lives of Helen, Juanita, Bryan, and Pastor Connie, as well as the lives of Bentley and his canine friend Daisy. But, ultimately, the flames were no match for their burning desires to live. The great fire within each of them could not be extinguished.

Meanwhile, Zack's burning desire for revenge – coupled with his drug-addled mind – had led him to commit a crime with more serious consequences than Abigail's battering, for which she had reported him to the police. His attempt to scare Abigail by torching the place where she was volunteering was senseless. The fire occurred while he was on probation for abusing Abigail. His lawyers privately conceded he would end up behind bars for the arson.

Zack's father, a major builder and developer in Arizona, would easily deal with the losses of the three partially built houses that Zack accidentally set on fire by carelessly disposing of a cigarette. But his father would find it difficult to deal with the Tucson community's outrage over his son's setting fire to a home for elderly ladies.

Still unable to sleep, Bentley kept thinking about having the great fire within, as Mei-Li had termed it, or about having the determination to accomplish something, as Josephine and Lara had put it.

Bentley was determined to cross Rainbow Bridge someday and be reunited with his first companion. He understood that in order for that to happen, he would have to serve the Indigo Bush residents in whatever way he could and for as long as he imagined Miss Lucy thought necessary. He wondered how he now could help his part-time home recover from the arson fire. He drifted into dreamland without an answer, but one would come soon enough.

Next: A Blue Christmas

Bentley and the Great Fire

A Christmas cactus in bloom, at right, and other holiday trappings fail to cheer up Bentley amid the financial anxiety at the Indigo Bush care home.

Paw Prints: With the arsonist having surrendered to the police, Bentley has turned his attention to the remaining immediate problem facing his part-time home – how to turn a dream for the future into reality.

Chapter 14 – A Blue Christmas

It was the day before Bentley's first Christmas without Miss Lucy.

Bentley sorely missed his first companion, who passed away about six months ago. His sadness reflected his loss, but it also mirrored the cheerlessness surrounding him at his part-time home.

Despite the traditional green-and-red holiday decorations (including potted Christmas cactus plants in full bloom), it was a blue Christmas at the Indigo Bush Assisted Living and Residential Care Home.

Bentley's current companions – the home's head administrator and its head chef – were putting up a brave front, but Julieta and Bryan privately acknowledged that Julieta's vision for Indigo Bush's future was fading away.

The care home's residents, its staff and the board of directors for the foundation that oversaw the home all liked Julieta's idea of replacing the old, fire-damaged building with a new, larger home, but the necessary funds to turn that dream into reality were nowhere to be found.

To put it simply, as Julieta did when she talked with Bryan on the ride with Bentley to the care home on the morning before Christmas, the care home needed a miracle.

"So we have some money, and there are grants that we

could apply for," Bryan said while driving. "But we really need to come up with a ton of cash soon to jump-start this whole thing."

"Like I just told you," said Julieta, "we need a miracle."

Seeking one that morning was Juanita. She was at Mission San Xavier del Bac, where she pinned a brass key to the blanket draped over the reclining statue of her patron saint. The *milagro* was the key to her room's old door, which was damaged in the fire and had been replaced. She had been taken to the church in a car driven by her grandson, who lived in Sierra Vista and was stationed at Fort Huachuca.

That morning, meanwhile, the man affectionately known as the Chief was among a small group of experienced climbers at Baboquivari Peak, southwest of Tucson. The Chief, who was a member of the Tohono O'odham Nation, was an Indigo Bush volunteer who played the piano during the weekly singalongs at the care home. He was climbing the 7,730-foot mountain, the home of the O'odham Indians' creator, I'itoi (commonly pronounced EE-ee-toy). The Chief was headed to a remote cave to seek the aid of Elder Brother, as I'itoi was also known. The Chief would sense the spirit of the sacred figure and pray in behalf of the residents and staff of the Indigo Bush care home in their time of need.

Meanwhile, south of Tucson in Green Valley, Pastor Connie added Indigo Bush's name to the names of needy members of her congregation in her prayer of intercession.

Not all the appeals in behalf of Indigo Bush that day were spiritual. Julieta's brother, José, bought an Arizona Lottery ticket in hopes of winning the Powerball jackpot, which he planned to turn over to his sister for the care home.

Despite the worrisome atmosphere, Christmas Eve at Indigo Bush was not without its diversions. For example, Helen and Ruth had their second annual early-evening viewing of Ruth's video of "It's a Wonderful Life," with Xenia, Vivien, Juanita, and Maria joining them this time.

Bentley, who had seen the classic movie before with Miss Lucy, wandered around the care home, but he did make it a point to return in time for his favorite scene – when George Bailey discovers that Zuzu's flower petals were indeed in his pocket, and thus, his life had been worth living.

A little while later, Bentley went with Julieta and Bryan to José's home, where Bentley watched Julieta's niece Gabriella use powdered sugar and cinnamon to make snowflakes out of flour tortillas. Even though José and his wife Elena were in the tortilla-making business, they and their relatives still made tortillas (soft and warm with a few burnt edges) as part of their holiday celebrations at home.

Across town, two sixth-graders were getting an early Christmas present from their parents.

"He's so cool," Clyde said, holding the 20-pound boxer puppy in his arms.

"We'll take care of him for sure," Callie said, patting the head of the new addition to their family.

The parents of the twin brother and sister had purchased the 3½-month-old dog from a breeder in Douglas, near the Mexico border. The pooch's color was fawn – a pale, yellowish brown – and his breeder had named him Mugsy.

Elsewhere in Tucson, Tyler was carrying pine cones from a sack in his family's garage. The boy was bringing them to his dad Tony, who was waiting in front of their fireplace. Tony would put the cones into the inner hearth and then put the wood on top of them. After the cones were lighted and the fire spread to the wood, it was time for Tyler, his dad and his mom Lola to exchange gifts.

Later that Christmas Eve, Abigail was exchanging gifts with her parents in the living room of their Santa Catalina Foothills home after the teenager returned from a party at her friends Nora and Sam's home, which was nearby.

Also nearby was the residence of Zack and his father,

who was divorced. They spent the evening arguing again about Zack's behavior. No gifts were exchanged in the undecorated hacienda, although the burly man had pointed out to the burly teenager that he had posted the hefty bail money for his son.

    Several miles away, in his workshop near his home, the man affectionately known as Mr. Fix-it was still working on the gift he would give Helen. Indigo Bush's volunteer handyman had phoned her that afternoon, and they had agreed to exchange presents on Christmas Day.

    Back across town later that night, Bentley was munching on a tortilla while Julieta and Bryan were kissing under the mistletoe in their home. For the moment, a blue Christmas wasn't so blue, after all.

    Nevertheless, Bentley knew Indigo Bush was only taking a holiday from facing its immediate problem. He wished Miss Lucy or Sasha could somehow help him again. Then he remembered Mei-Li's story about the fire within, and he thought about being prepared to do whatever he had to do when the opportunity arose.

Next: "A New Beginning"

On leashes, Bentley and Daisy join Helen and Mr. Fix-it at the confetti-sprinkled groundbreaking. Bentley uses his paw to mark the occasion.

🐾 *Paw Prints: With Julieta's vision for Indigo Bush's future dimming, Bentley has been looking for a way to have the fire within him brighten the outlook of the care home's head administrator. Clearly, Bentley now sees there is little time left to keep her vision from vanishing.* 🐾

Chapter 15 – "A New Beginning"

It was New Year's Eve. It also was 60 days since the fire at the care home. And it was 11 days since the arsonist surrendered. To Bentley and his buddies at the care home, however, it was a relatively short while before the zero hour.

Oh sure, there was an early-evening party going on in the care home's activity room, which was radiantly decorated to welcome 2004. But the home's fund-raising shortfall had overshadowed the celebration.

Actually, a more accurate description for the deficiency would be a new word – "longfall." Indigo Bush wasn't anywhere close to having the money needed to turn Julieta's vision into reality. The care home had received numerous donations from the Tucson community and had begun to line up grant money, but there had been no tremendous financial jump-start for the plan to replace the old building with a new, expanded home.

The board of directors for the foundation that oversaw Indigo Bush had hoped for an extremely wealthy benefactor to provide the jump-start before the end of the calendar year, but no one with extremely deep pockets had come forward. So the directors were fully expecting to put the plan for the new home on hold – indefinitely. Actually, the exact word would be "definitely," as in *definitely* no new home for the foreseeable future.

But the board's decision would have to wait for the new year. At the moment, the old year was still hanging on, and it was time to party.

In the care home's activity room, Julieta was dancing her cares away with her husband, Bryan. She enjoyed fox trotting with Indigo Bush's head chef, whose dance card held the names of a dozen of the care home's ladies.

Among the three other dancing couples were Helen and the volunteer handyman known as Mr. Fix-it. Helen and Mr. Fix-it weren't actually trotting, rather they were shuffling along. Helen was mindful of her recuperation from heart surgery, and Mr. Fix-it was mindful of his "two left feet" (actually, he was a good dancer; he was only kidding Helen).

Not far from the dancing couples, another couple was doing a dance of sorts near Pastor Connie. Bentley and Daisy were playfully scampering around, their tails wagging.

Suddenly, the music ended. The piano man, known affectionately as the Chief, stopped playing when he saw the burly teenager and the burly man. They had been escorted into the activity room by the care home's receptionist, a volunteer from the Volunteer Center of Southern Arizona.

"Excuse us," the burly man said in a loud voice to his stunned audience. "We don't mean to be crashing your party, but we have something to say," he added, turning toward the burly teenager. "I'm sure you all know who I am, but here is my son, Zack. He wants to have a word."

Zack awkwardly stepped forward and nervously pursed his lips. He took a deep breath and exhaled. "I want to apologize to each and every one of you for what I did," he said in an earnest voice. "Abigail, again I am especially sorry," he added, glancing at the red-haired volunteer who had been serving the orange-sherbet punch at the party. Then he looked at Bentley and Daisy and managed a weak smile.

"As his father, I, too, want to apologize for this terrible tragedy," Zack's father hastily added. "Zack will accept whatever punishment he receives. He will receive counseling . . . I . . . will receive counseling with him. I . . ."

Zack's father was at a loss for further words. His audience remained stunned. There was absolute silence. Zack's father lowered his head, and his son did likewise.

Then, from across the room, there came a friendly face, which was what Zack and his father had been looking for. The face was Bentley's.

BENTLEY AND THE GREAT FIRE / CH. 15 - "A NEW BEGINNING"

With his tail wagging, Bentley walked up to Zack and raised his front paws onto Zack's right pant leg, prompting the surprised teenager to pat Bentley's head. Then, Bentley did likewise with Zack's father and got the same response.

"So you are the Bentley I've heard about," Zack's father said, breaking the long silence. "You're wonderful."

"Yes, he is!" shouted Helen, surprising herself at having spoken up.

"We can all be proud of him," Julieta said, stepping forward. "He knows how to greet visitors," she added, continuing to walk toward Zack and his father. She introduced herself to them and shook hands with them. "We accept your apologies. Thank you for coming tonight."

"Thank you," Zack's father said quickly. "And to show our appreciation, we have something for you," he added, handing a piece of paper to Julieta. "It's a new beginning."

Julieta glanced at the check and couldn't believe her eyes. She was flabbergasted. "I . . . I don't know how to . . . thank you," she managed to mutter. "Thank you. Thank you."

"You can thank this little guy here, too," Zack said, smiling as he patted Bentley's right shoulder.

Julieta turned around and flashed a megawatt smile while holding up the amazing check in her right hand.

"Happy New Year!" she squealed, unable to contain her happiness. Her brother José had not won the Powerball lottery, but she had just received a Powerball-sized check from one of Arizona's wealthiest developers. "It's going to be a great new year for all of us," she added, her excitement prompting several ladies to walk toward her and join the impromptu celebration.

    Later, after all the oohing and aahing subsided and after Zack and his father had sipped orange-sherbet punch and said goodbye, a few of the ladies speculated that Zack's father had acted to stem the bad publicity he had faced, or to somehow save on his taxes, or to help himself in yet another way.

    Regardless of his motive, Zack's father had jump-started the process that would lead to a new Indigo Bush.

    Just before the time when Tyler's family and Gabriella's family and most other families in Arizona would begin their New Year's Eve parties, Helen went to her room to get Bentley's leash. She smiled again as she looked at the large, copper Southwestern-style picture frame that Mr. Fix-it had given her as a Christmas gift (the retired professional photographer gave him a half-dozen photographs that she had taken of his beloved B-24 at the Pima Air & Space Museum).

    Bentley was leashed as he walked beside Helen. They met up with Mr. Fix-it, who was with a leashed Daisy. They all walked past the room of Mei-Li, who was sitting in her chair 22 days before the Chinese Lunar New Year and doing a yogic hum (at 100 years young, she still was interested in the doings of the Arizona Yoga Association).

After heading outdoors, Helen and Mr. Fix-it led Bentley and Daisy to the prickly pear cactus patch behind the care home. It was Helen's idea to have a symbolic groundbreaking for the new Indigo Bush.

Bentley looked up at the sky and wondered about Miss Daisy and about Sasha. He hoped that by drawing on the fire within him to break the icy silence at the party, he had shown them that he had understood what Mei-Li meant about the Green Dragon's ability to do good for others.

"Here goes!" shouted Helen, digging into the ground with the small trowel that Mr. Fix-it had brought from the storage shed near the garden behind the care home.

"That's a start," Mr. Fix-it said, smiling and giving Helen a gentle hug before sprinkling confetti on the ground.

Bentley brushed noses with Daisy. Then he lifted his right paw and scraped the ground twice. And once more for good measure.

The End

Acknowledgments

This story's recognition of the power of determination is a tribute to the perseverance that God's creations are capable of drawing from within themselves to face adversity.

As was the case with the first book in the *Bentley Book Series,* many people contributed in many ways to this sequel. Foremost was my wife Connie – my co-illustrator and primary source of inspiration. This book would not have been possible without her hard work and dedication, particularly in computer compositing and page design. My other co-illustrator, Guillermo Munro, helped produce illustrations that are creative, colorful, and wondrous.

My father-in-law, Virgil Falkner, continued to be a source of inspiration and information; he also gave his permission to photograph his cabin for Chapter 8. My stepson, firefighter Brian Anspach, provided technical information, and also gave his permission to photograph his pickup truck for Chapter 12. My stepdaughter, Angela Anspach, continued to serve as a creative consultant and vital contributor. My niece Barbara (Mrs. Kevin Brown, nee Pintozzi) provided proofreading assistance. Others who helped included Brian's wife, Julie; and my siblings (Anne-Marie, Charles, and Anthony) and their spouses (George Cina, Rose Marie and Maureen, respectively); and dear friends Mr. and Mrs. Grant and Doris Blum and Mr. and Mrs. Anthony and Lola Iacullo. Also contributing to this story were fond memories of my parents, Mr. and Mrs. Charles and Maria Pintozzi; and mother-in-law, Mrs. Lucille Falkner.

Also helping were several of my Arizona Daily Star co-workers, including Lupe Ortiz, Linda Velazquez, Elaine Raines and Dave Skog, who served as my unofficial focus group. Angela Soto shared her artistic creativity by providing the mosaic-tile table in Chapter 11. Anthony Broadman's Oct. 30, 2003, article on The Day of the Dead was a source of information, as was Doug Kreutz's Nov. 30, 2003, article on the Tohono O'odham creator, I'itoi.

Holocaust survivor Stephen Nasser's Feb. 15, 2004, speech in Tucson inspired the recollection in Chapter 13.

Janet Wood, manager of the Newspapers in Education program, served as a source of encouragement for this book.

Representatives of the Tucson-area organizations mentioned in this story also were informative resources. The Pima Air & Space Museum cooperated with my photographic requests for Chapter 7.

Public relations consultants Andrew T. Greeley and Casey DeLorme again provided insightful comments.

The ladies of St. Luke's Home continued to be a real-life inspiration (in particular, fond memories of Xenia Kawchack and Vivien Monahan).

Finally, the real-life Bentley continued to be a most cooperative photographic model, as well as an inspirational role model. (All the paw prints in this book are actually his.)

– Nick Pintozzi

Behind the Scenes

Nick Pintozzi is a copy editor at the Arizona Daily Star, in Tucson, Arizona. He and his wife, Connie, share their home with three Chihuahuas. They are members of the Society of Southwestern Authors, the Arizona Book Publishing Association, and the Society of Children's Book Writers & Illustrators.

Guillermo Munro, former graphics director at the Arizona Daily Star, is working at a publication in the American Northwest and also studying fine art.

Community Outreach

(List of organizations by order of appearance in
"Bentley and the Great Fire")

Humane Society of Southern Arizona
www.humane-so-arizona.org

Tucson Fire Department
www.cityoftucson.org/fire/

Tucson Chinese Association
www.tucsonchinese.org

Pan Asian Community Alliance
www.azstarnet.com/~vna/organizations/panasian.htm

Tucson Children's Museum
www.tucsonchildrensmuseum.org

Patronato San Xavier
www.patronatosanxavier.org

Tucson Police Department
www.ci.tucson.az.us/police/

Pima Council on Aging
www.pcoa.org

Pima County Juvenile Court
www.pcjcc.co.pima.az.us

Pima Air & Space Museum
www.pimaair.org

American Red Cross Southern Arizona Chapter
www.tucson-redcross.org

Pima County Attorney's Office's 88-CRIME hotline
www.pcao.co.pima.az.us/88crime.shtml

Fox Tucson Theatre Foundation
www.foxtucsontheatre.org

Community Food Bank
www.communityfoodbank.com

Southern Arizona Chapter of the Arthritis Foundation
www.arthritis.org

Desert Southwest Chapter of the Alzheimer's Association
www.alzdsw.org

Dunbar Coalition
    Dunbar Alumni Association
    Dunbar/Spring Neighborhood Association
    Juneteenth Festival Committee
    Tucson Urban League
www.thedunbarproject.com

Tucson Arizona Boys Chorus
www.boyschorus.org

Ballet Folklórico San Juan
www.users.qwest.net/~juliegallego/sanjuan.html

Jewish Family & Children's Service of Southern Arizona's Holocaust Survivor Group
www.jfcstucson.org/holocaust_services.htm

Volunteer Center of Southern Arizona
www.volunteersoaz.org

Arizona Yoga Association
www.azyoga.com

Bentley and the Great Fire

Coming next . . .

Bentley and the Monstrous Monsoon

autumn 2005

To order books in the Bentley Book Series, contact your local bookstore or please visit:

www.bentleythedog.com
(the site includes photos, games, and other fun)

To obtain an order form by mail, please contact:

BentDaiSha, LLC
11020 E. Indigo Bush Place
Tucson, AZ 85748